The Park

by Helen Gregory

Consultant:
Adria F. Klein, Ph.D.
California State University, San Bernardino

capstone
classroom

Heinemann Raintree • Red Brick Learning
division of Capstone

It is time to go to the park.

We can play at the park.

We can sit and talk at the park.

We can smell flowers at the park.

We can walk on a path at the park.

We can sit on a bench at the park.

We can feed the animals at the park.

We can feed the fish
at the park.

We can climb at the park.

We can swing at the park.

We can bike at the park.

We can slide at the park.

We can have a snack at the park.

We can roast marshmallows at the park.

We can have a birthday party at the park!